AMAZING ANIMAL MINDS

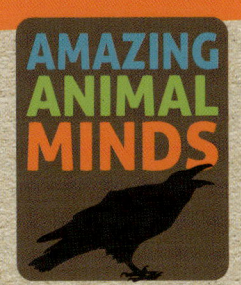

ELEPHANTS

by Joyce Markovics

CHERRY LAKE PRESS
Ann Arbor, Michigan

CHERRY LAKE PRESS

Published in the United States of America by Cherry Lake Publishing
Ann Arbor, Michigan
www.cherrylakepublishing.com

Reading Adviser: Beth Walker Gambro, MS, Ed., Reading Consultant, Yorkville, IL
Content Adviser: Rachel Morrison, PhD, Animal Behavior Scientist
Book Designer: Ed Morgan

Photo Credits: freepik.com, cover and title page; © Images of Africa Photobank/Alamy Stock Photo, 5; © Vladimir Turkenich/Shutterstock, 6–7; © MarcelClemens/Shutterstock, 8; © GoodFocused/Shutterstock, 9; © Boonrod/Shutterstock, 10; © John Michael Vosloo/Shutterstock, 11; Courtesy of Dr. Preston Foerder and Dr. Diana Reiss, 12; © Joshua Plotnik, Richard Lair, and Frans de Waal, 13; © nathapolHPS/Shutterstock, 14–15; freepik.com, 17; freepik.com, 18; © Joshua Plotnik, 19; freepik.com, 20–21; © Adam Ferguson and Joshua Plotnik, 22.

Copyright © 2024 by Cherry Lake Publishing Group

All rights reserved. No part of this book may be reproduced or utilized in any form or by any means without written permission from the publisher.

Cherry Lake Press is an imprint of Cherry Lake Publishing Group.

Library of Congress Cataloging-in-Publication Data has been filed and is available at catalog.loc.gov.

Printed in the United States of America by
Corporate Graphics

Note from publisher: Websites change regularly, and their future contents are outside of our control. Supervise children when conducting any recommended online searches for extended learning opportunities.

CONTENTS

Elephant Grief 4
Brains and Trunks 8
Smart and Social 12
Saving Elephants 20

Scientist Spotlight 22
Glossary 23
Find Out More 24
Index 24
About the Authors 24

ELEPHANT GRIEF

In 2013, scientist Shifra Goldenberg was studying elephants in Kenya when tragedy struck. A female African elephant named Queen Victoria died. The elephant was the **matriarch** of her family group.

Then a few weeks after her death, something surprising happened. Three different elephant families, including Victoria's own family, visited her dead body. They lingered over her **carcass**. The elephants stroked her skull with their trunks. They gently touched her bones. Shifra was floored.

Elephants in Africa examine the bones of a dead elephant. They sometimes cover a carcass with leaves and sticks as if to bury it.

Elephants are the largest animals that live on land. These huge **mammals** can weigh up to 7.5 tons (6.8 metric tons).

"What the [elephant] family was doing was interesting," said Shifra. "But what her **nonrelatives** were doing is also important." Shifra shot a video showing the elephants touching Victoria's body. "It is amazing to see that level of fascination," she said.

Shifra was left wondering: What was going through the elephants' minds? They seem to understand death. And they appear to experience the loss as grief—similar to humans. After studying elephants for decades, scientists are just beginning to learn what's inside their incredible minds.

> There are three known types of elephants. Two larger species live in Africa. The third smaller species makes its home in Asia.

7

BRAINS AND TRUNKS

Grief is one of many signs that elephants have complex minds. They can think, communicate, and experience emotions. Elephants can function at a high level due in part to their brains. So how big is an elephant's brain? Huge! It's about three to four times larger than a human brain. But it's not the size that matters. Parts of an elephant's brain are larger and more complex than other mammal brains. These areas help an elephant sense and experience the world in a **unique** way.

A male elephant's skull

8

An elephant's skull weighs about 115 pounds (52 kilograms)! It must be large enough to protect the animal's big brain.

The brain controls everything, including an elephant's most important senses: smell and touch. An elephant uses its trunk to both smell and touch. The trunk is strong enough to push down trees. It's also **agile** enough to grab a piece of grass.

An elephant can use its trunk the same way a person uses their hands. But it can lift much heavier things!

It can take months for baby elephants to learn how to use their trunks.

An elephant's trunk is also a nose. It has two **nostrils** that carry air to the lungs. The trunk can also suck up water but not like a straw. It holds the water before squirting it into the elephant's mouth. In addition, the trunk can sniff out a **predator** and find food.

> An elephant's trunk is an **elongated** nose and upper lip. The trunk is also used to greet and caress other elephants.

SMART AND SOCIAL

In 2010, Kandula, an elephant at the National Zoo in Washington, DC, smelled something delicious with his trunk. Yet the tasty treat was in a tree out of reach. So Kandula marched over to a large plastic cube in his pen. Using his trunk, he pushed it beneath the tree. Then the smart elephant used the cube as a step stool to grab the treat!

Kandula the elephant stands on a cube to reach for food above his head. Kandula also taught himself how to stack blocks to reach a snack.

Kandula had no idea he was being watched by a team of scientists, including Diana Reiss. Diana studies elephants and other animals. "It's fascinating to try and find ways of testing animals' minds so they can show us what they are really capable of," said Diana.

Elephants working together to access a treat

In another **experiment** carried out by scientist Joshua Plotnik and others, pairs of elephants cooperated to get food. The food was placed on a sliding table with one rope around it. To reach the treat, the elephants had to each pull one end of the rope at the same time. They quickly learned that if they didn't work together, neither one got food!

Scientists have seen elephants solve problems in many ways. They use sticks and other tools to remove or swat bugs on their skin. Elephants also pick up rocks and logs. Sometimes, they toss things while playing. One time, an elephant chucked a sandal at the scientist who was researching her!

In Asia, elephants and people often work closely together. One story tells of an elephant that was setting logs in holes. Suddenly, he stopped while holding the log above the hole. The **mahout** ordered the elephant to keep working. But he refused. The human looked in the hole and found a dog sleeping in it! Only after the dog moved would the elephant put the log into the hole.

Elephants also show **foresight**. In Africa, an elephant was spotted drinking fresh water from a hole in the ground. When he was done, he plugged the hole with bark and sand. The elephant later went back to the hole, unplugged it, and drank more water.

Elephants are also known for their complex social behavior. Most live in groups, or herds. Herds are made up of related females and their young. The herd's leader is the matriarch. She and her family are closely bonded. They use **body language** and calls to stay in constant contact with each other.

All the adults help take care of the young and each other. They seem to understand when another animal is in distress. This is called **empathy**. For example, elephants help comfort and **reunite** lost calves with their mothers. They care for injured and sick elephants. They will even feed an ill elephant that can't feed itself. And they appear to **mourn** their dead.

Elephants comfort each other by chirping softly and using their trunks to touch or stroke one another.

"Being part of an elephant family is all about unity and working together for the greater good," said Joyce Poole, elephant expert.

Part of being social is having a good memory. Elephants can remember hundreds of different faces. Zoo elephants can easily tell their keepers from other staff. They can even recognize other elephants after decades of being apart. Elephants also seem to remember very good or bad experiences, just like humans.

Year after year, elephants can remember the exact locations of water holes hundreds of miles apart.

Elephants have another special ability. They can recognize themselves in mirrors! Being self-aware is another sign of intelligence. When most animals see their **reflection** in a mirror, they think it's another animal. But not elephants. To test this idea, Joshua Plotnik put white marks on elephants' heads and gave them a mirror. Happy was the first elephant to recognize herself in the mirror. She repeatedly touched the mark—and even tried to wipe it off!

Not all elephants pass the mirror self-recognition test. Besides humans, other animals that recognize themselves in mirrors include great apes and dolphins and possibly a bird and fish species.

SAVING ELEPHANTS

Scientists now know that elephants are thinking and feeling beings. And these majestic creatures have abilities humans are just beginning to understand. However, for hundreds of years, elephants have been killed for their tusks. Today, elephants are protected. But **poachers** still slaughter them. On top of that, people have destroyed many of the wild places where elephants live.

While studying elephants, Joshua Plotnik is also fighting to save their **habitats**. "If we don't understand elephant behavior, we can't come up with good solutions for protecting them in the wild," said Joshua. "If we want elephants to continue to exist in the wild, we have to protect their habitat."

Many experts oppose keeping elephants in zoos. Why? Many zoos can't recreate the complex social lives of wild elephants. And zoo elephants often don't get enough exercise. On the plus side, many zoos support efforts to save elephants. And without zoos, few people would get to see an elephant up close.

SCIENTIST SPOTLIGHT

Joshua Plotnik

Joshua "Josh" Plotnik has devoted his life to learning about Asian elephants. He focuses his work on how elephants think and understand the world. To study these amazing animals, Josh observes them in the wild. He also develops tests to see how they solve problems. "You have to understand the animal that you are trying to protect," said Josh.

Josh is also passionate about teaching. "We use the study of elephants as a hook to get kids more interested in and to think more critically about science, and to be more **conscious** about how their decisions will impact the environment," said Josh. His hope is that more young people will take action to save elephants and their wild homes.

GLOSSARY

agile (AJ-il) able to move around easily and gracefully

body language (BOD-ee LANG-wij) a message suggested by the way an animal moves its body

carcass (KAR-kuhss) the dead body of an animal

conscious (KON-shuss) being aware and responsive

elongated (ih-LAWNG-geyt-uhd) long and thin

empathy (EM-puh-thee) the ability to understand and share the feelings of another

experiment (ek-SPER-uh-ment) a scientific test set up to find the answer to a question

foresight (FAWR-sahyt) the ability to predict something

habitats (HAB-uh-tats) places in the wild where animals normally live

mahout (muh-HOOT) a person in Southeast Asia who works with, rides, and cares for an elephant

mammals (MAM-uhlz) warm-blooded animals that have hair or fur and drink their mothers' milk

matriarch (MEY-tree-ahrk) the female leader of a family or group

mourn (MORN) to feel very sad about the loss of someone

nonrelatives (non-REL-uh-tivs) not related or connected by blood

nostrils (NOSS-truhlz) two openings in the nose that are used for breathing and smelling

poachers (POHCH-urz) people who hunt animals illegally

predator (PRED-uh-tur) an animal that hunts and kills other animals for food

reflection (ri-FLEKT-shun) an image seen in a mirror or shiny surface

reunite (ree-yoo-NITE) to bring together after being apart

unique (yoo-NEEK) one of a kind; like no other

FIND OUT MORE

BOOKS

Lloyd, Christopher. *Humanimal*. Greenbelt, MD: What on Earth Books, 2019.

Recio, Belinda. *Inside Animal Hearts and Minds*. New York, NY: Skyhorse Publishing, 2017.

Rish, Jocelyn. *Battle of the Brains: The Science Behind Animal Minds*. New York, NY: Running Press Kids, 2022.

WEBSITES

Explore these online sources with an adult:

Britannica Kids: Animal Behavior

PBS: The Emotional Lives of Animals

Think Elephants International

INDEX

brains, 8-10
cooperation, 13
death, 4, 6
elephant preservation, 20-22
empathy, 16
foresight, 15
Goldenberg, Shifra, 4, 6
grief, 4, 6, 8
habitat, 6, 20-21
Kandula, 12-13
memory, 18
mourning behavior, 4, 6, 16
Plotnik, Joshua, 13, 19, 21-22

poaching, 20
Poole, Joyce, 17
problem-solving abilities, 12-14
Reiss, Diana, 13
self-recognition (in mirrors), 19
skulls, 4, 8-9
smell, 10-11
social behavior, 16-18
tool use, 14
touch, 10
trunks, 4, 8, 10-12, 16
zoos, 12, 18, 21

ABOUT THE AUTHOR

Joyce Markovics has written hundreds of books for kids. She often thinks about what's going on inside the complex and sensitive mind of her pet rabbit, Babette. She hopes to learn how to speak "Bunny" one day. Joyce would like to extend an elephant-sized thanks to Josh Plotnick for his help with this book and his work to understand and protect elephants.